COLOR TEST PAGE

This Book Belongs To

_____

Halloween coloring book for kids ages 5-10

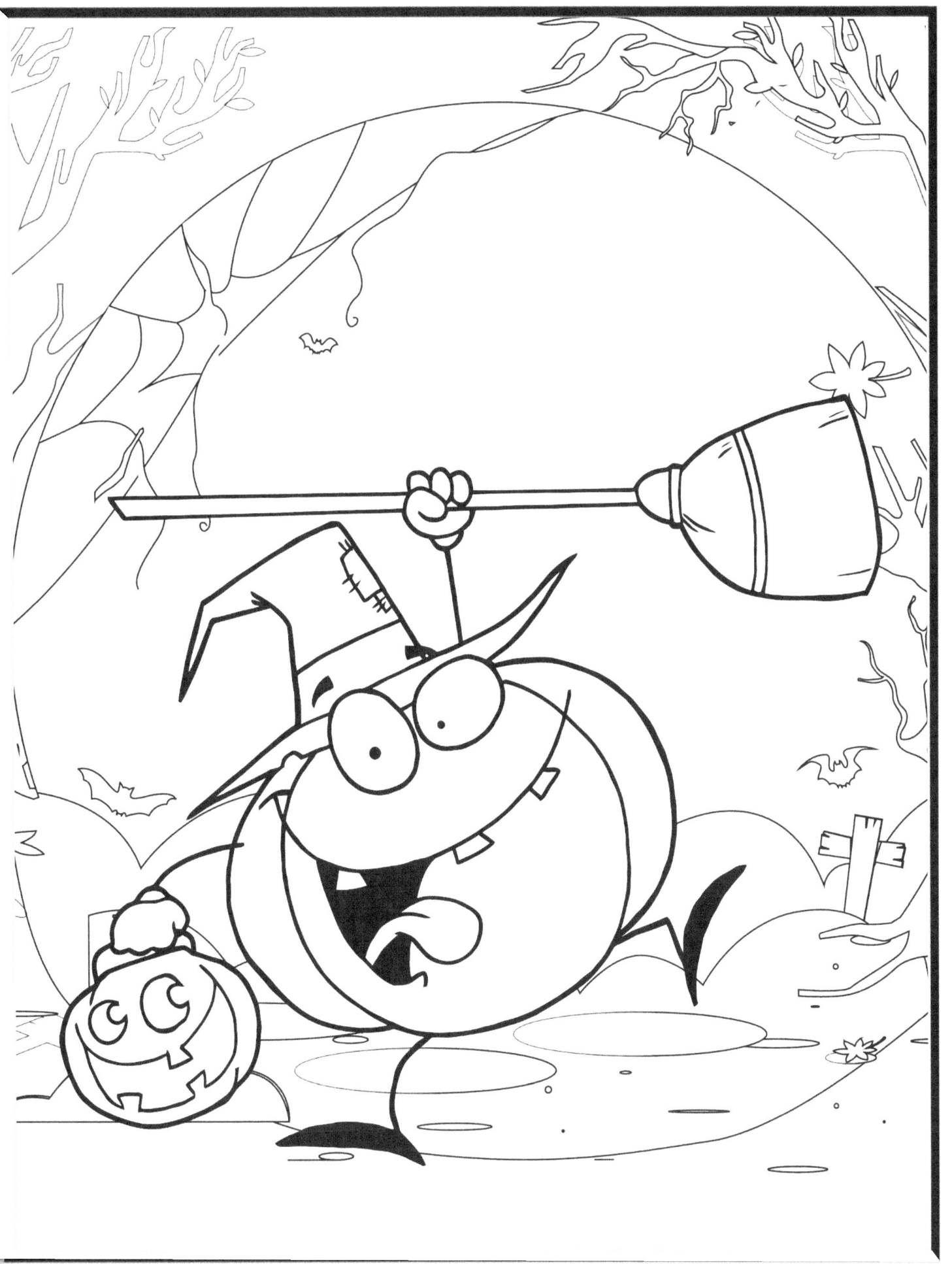

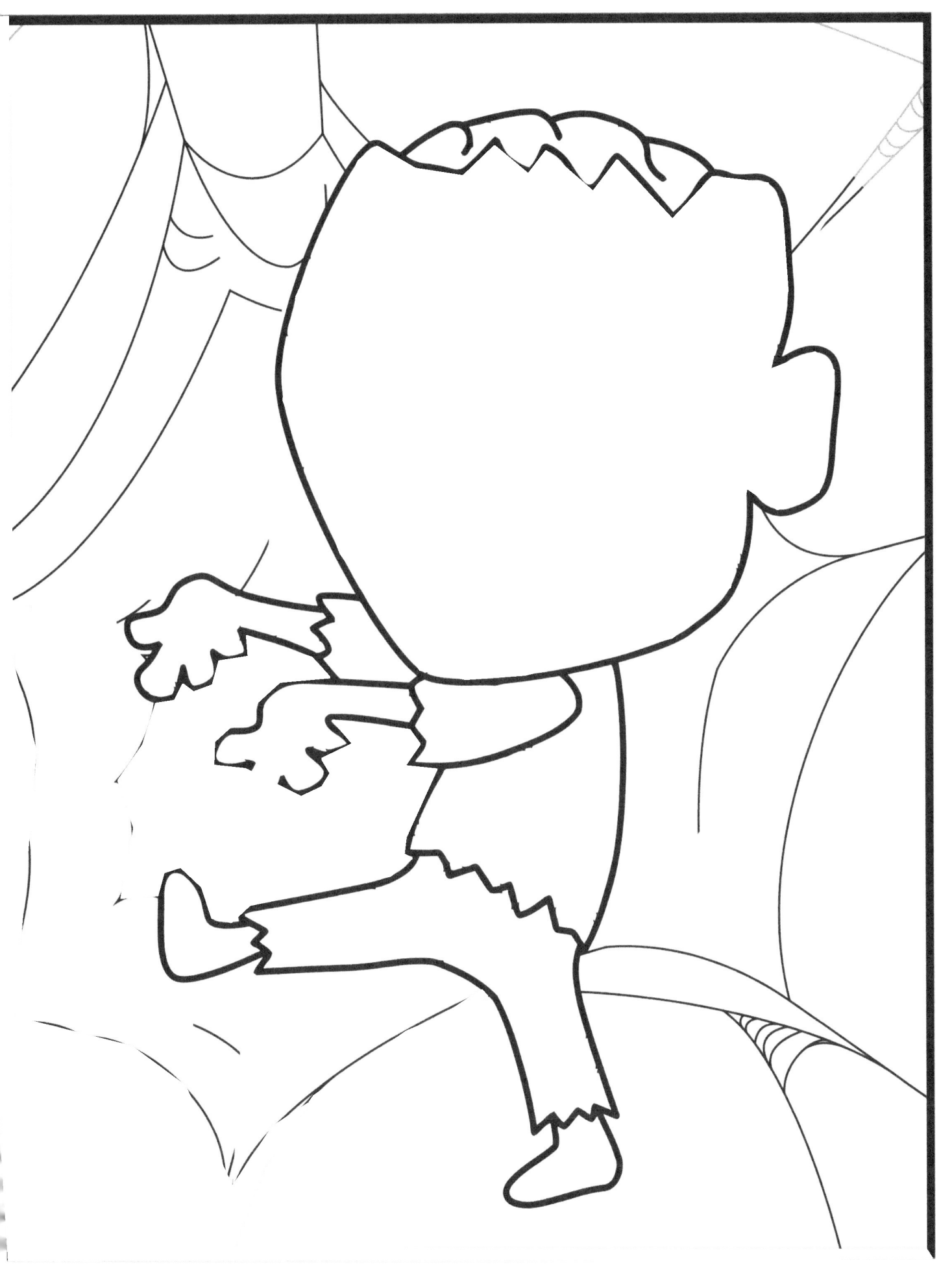

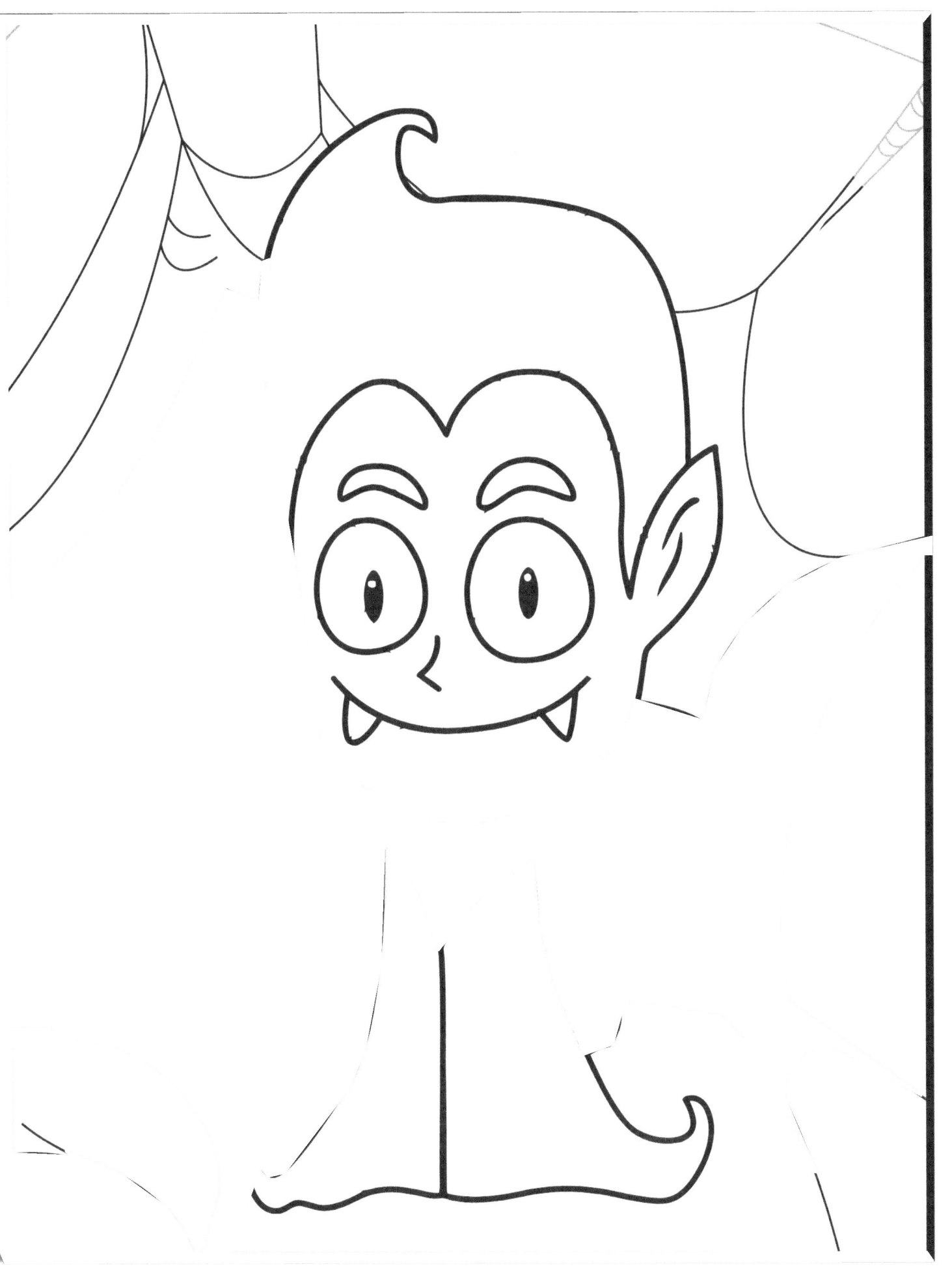

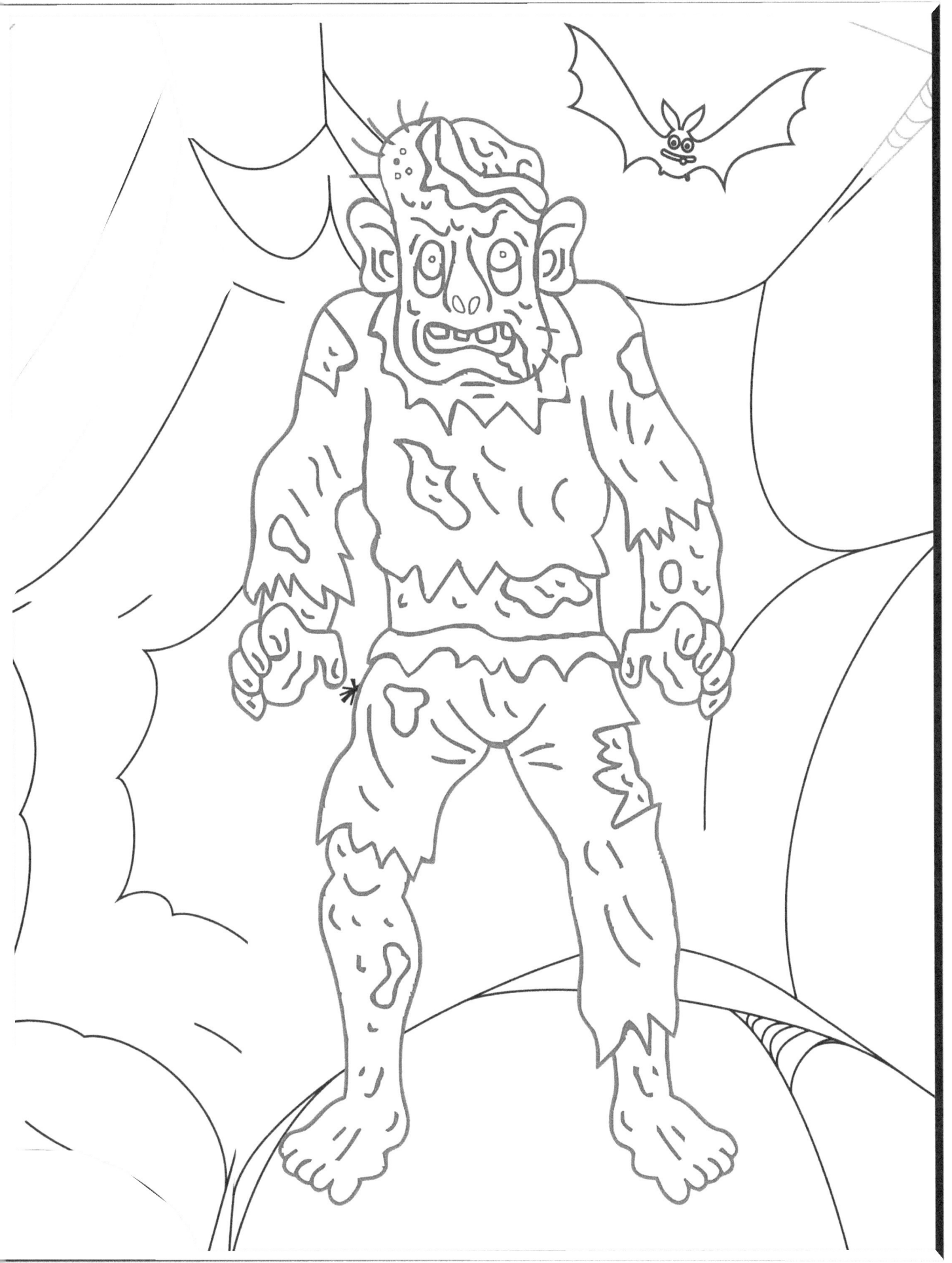

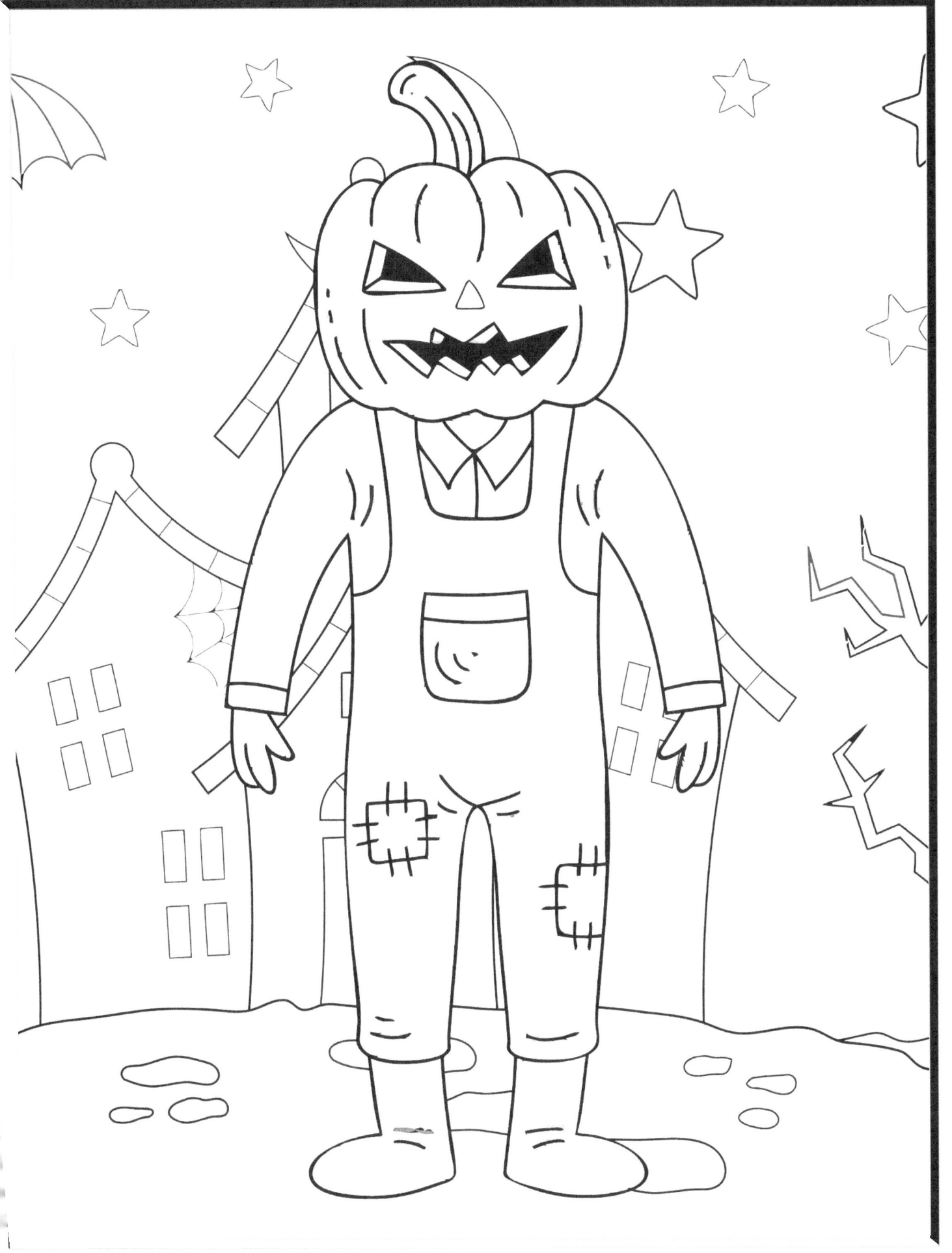

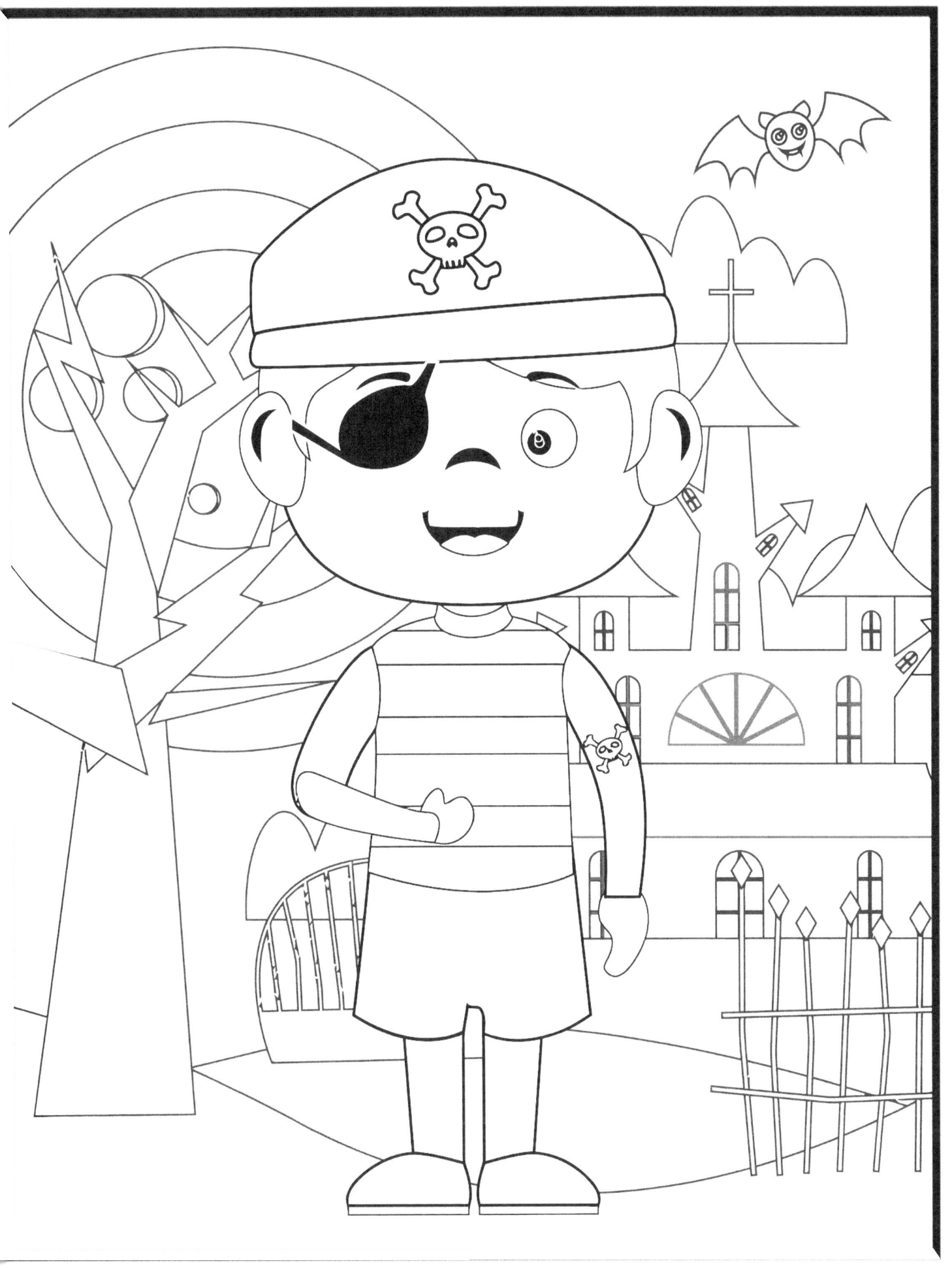

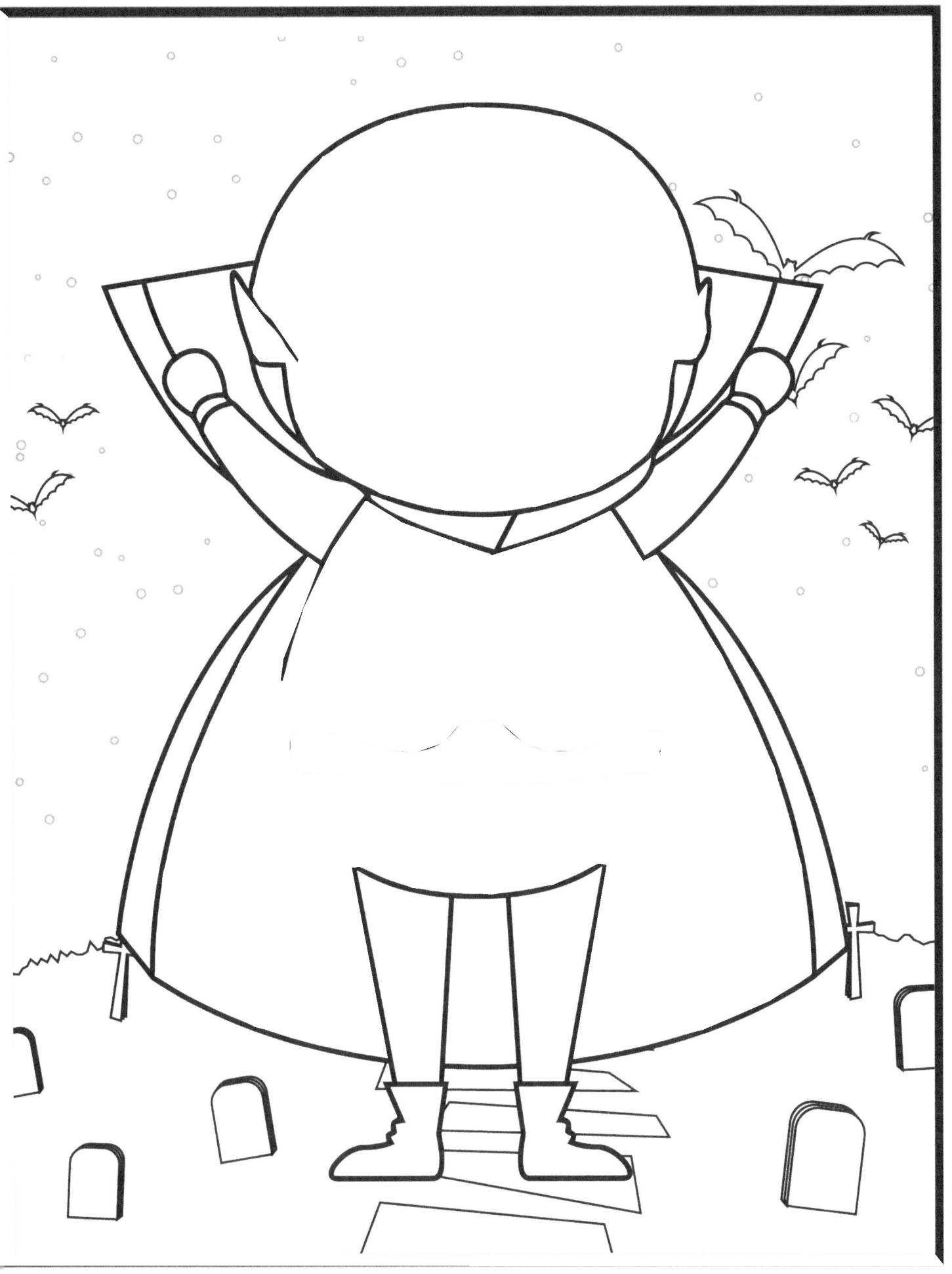

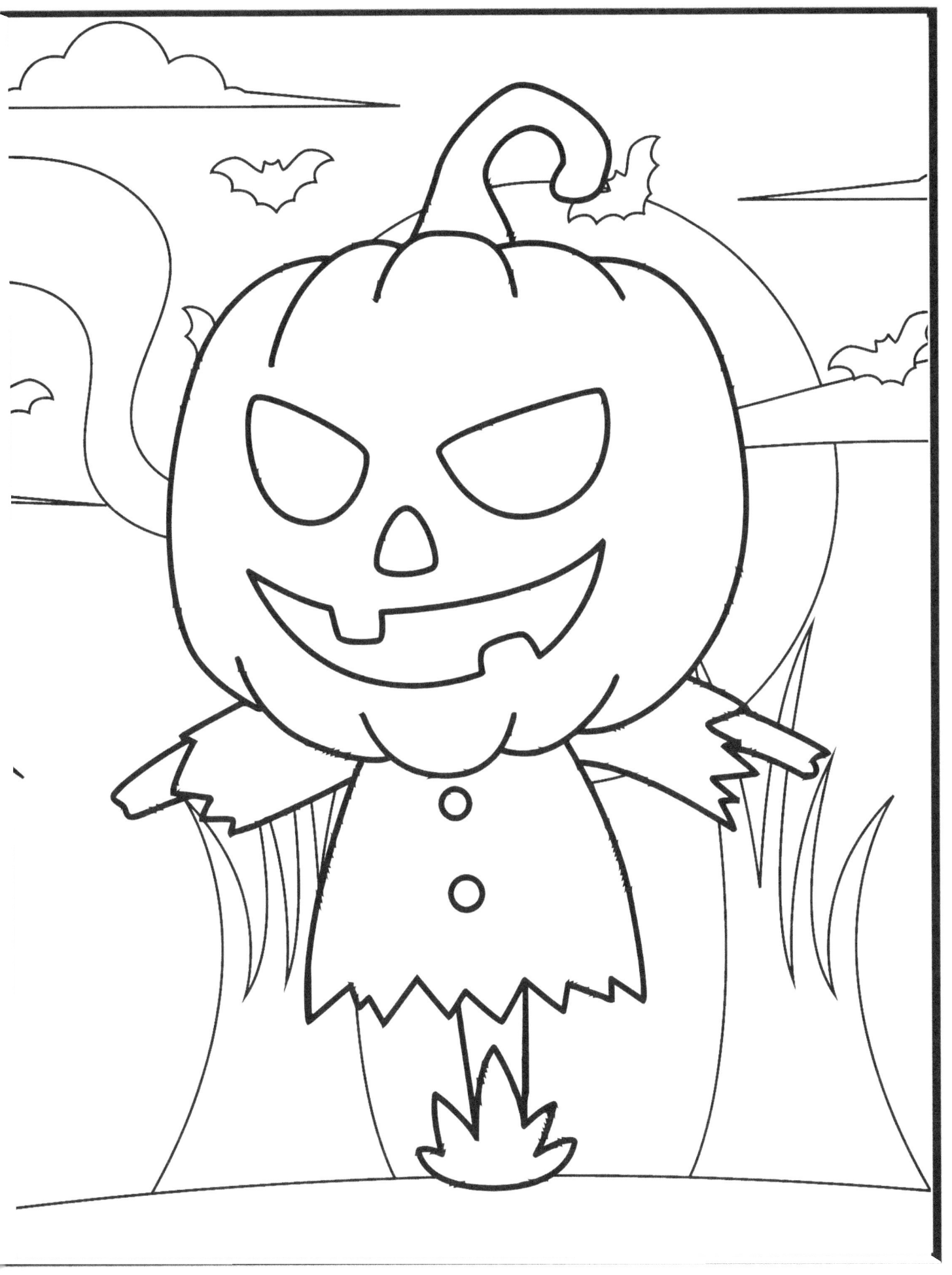

www.ingramcontent.com/pod-product-compliance
Lightning Source LLC
Chambersburg PA
CBHW060002230526
45472CB00008B/1909